Business vehicle
EIN ONLY

BOSSES BUILD BUSINESS CREDIT
VOLUME 3

PATRICE S JORDAN

Business Vehicle EIN ONLY

Business Development & No PG Business Credit
Patrice S. Jordan, No PG Business Credit Consultant
www.bossesbuildbusinesscredit.com

Copyright © 2024 by
Bosses Build Business Credit / Her Secret Vault Inc.

Key people to have as part of your business:

Renee Bobb, CEO of Renee Bobb Training LLC (https://reneebobbtraining.com/)
(Everything and more you need to know to win grants.)

Rosezena J. Pierce of RJ Pierce Law Group, P.C.
Trademark Attorney @thebizlawyer

ISBN: 979-8-9908768-0-4

Library of Congress Control Number: 2024914740

Printed in the United States

CONTENTS

DEDICATION

To my dearest daughter, Lily,

You are the light that guided me through my darkest times. Your birth gave me the strength I needed to escape a life of domestic violence. Without you, I might not have had the courage to leave, or worse, I might not be here today. This book is for you, my love. I am forever grateful and endlessly proud to be your mother. I love you and thank you from the depths of my heart.

I also want to express my deepest gratitude to God. Thank you for carrying me through those challenging moments and placing me in a position where I can now extend a helping hand to those in need. Your guidance and strength have been my foundation.

ACKNOWLEDGMENTS

I would like to extend my heartfelt gratitude to those who have played significant roles in my journey.

First and foremost, to my sister, Louett Brown, thank you for providing me with a couch to sleep on when I needed it the most. Your support and kindness during my toughest times have been invaluable.

To my parents, Louis Jordan and Patricia Lowery, thank you for giving me life and for your unwavering love and support.

I want to acknowledge my top students, Latasha Jackson and Monai Dupree-King. Latasha, with fourteen vehicles under your business, and Monai, with twelve vehicles under your business, you both exemplify the success and determination that inspire many.

Most importantly, to my community, thank you for allowing me to lead you into continuous success. Your trust and support have been the foundation of my mission to empower and uplift.

WHAT TO EXPECT
FROM THIS BOOK

—————⊃⊂⊃⊂⊃⊂—————

"Hi, everyone! Yesterday I was approved for a 2022 Mercedes A220. The process was so easy, and I was approved within ten minutes! The dealership said I was the first person to get financed with no PG, and they were so amazed. All glory to God and thank you to Patrice Jordan for teaching all of us! God bless you, Patrice! I'm so grateful! My life will never be the same!" – *Priya Moses*

"Patrice S. Jordan, I want to thank you from the bottom of my heart for equipping me with the tools to lead my family to financial freedom! I found you last year and informed my family. Only one person took heed and that was my little sister. I did a consultation with you and explained to you what I wanted for my family. I brought my sister along with me to the Dallas Business Boss Summit, and, as a gift for her birthday, I purchased her the book you had for sale today. She walked away with a brand new 2022 Mercedes-Benz! NO PG, NO DOWN PAYMENT! We thank you!

I have a video for you as well! She's set, and I'm grateful I'm next." – *Tina Hi*

"Toot! I sat in the vehicle challenge on December 21st—five whole mind-blowing days of information to start anew. This is my second vehicle in three weeks. I am getting this listed by Tuesday on four platforms. I am so grateful for Patrice S. Jordan and her mindset. You gave and gave us all you got. I studied and watched the videos for at least four sessions until I had my story straight. Still waiting for my Paydex score to populate. Until then, I am looking to find our next two luxury rides. By the way, we are doing Uber Black car until someone books this beauty. Everyone has encouraged me to jump out there." – *Tanya McNeal*

"So, guess what I did to gain my first employee? This car now works for the Galore Empire. Not a penny down with full coverage insurance at $60 a month (commercial). Thanks, Patrice S. Jordan. You are so amazing and have changed my life forever. Business credit on point." – *BIG PORSCHE DreDrei Pope*

"When I say that Coach P is the truth @Her Secret Vault Inc., just follow the blueprint and remember that #bossesbuildbusinesscredit. I got approved on my first try. NO PG, NO MONEY DOWN, 2019 Mercedes C Class." – *Evelyn Blake*

"Thank you coach for everything. You helped me beat these games. So let me tell y'all. I went to this dealership three weeks ago and got denied with another business because my business said CAR RENTAL. So I said, 'Let me start over.' I got a new business on February 18, 2022, and I got approved for this car on March 25, 2022. I don't have a Paydex score at all. Remember, my business is new. I'm not even done with tier 1 yet and got approved for a $54,000 car. But I remember everything coach said and went for it. I got approved three minutes later. No PG at all! This was at Toyota in South Atlanta. Thank you again, coach." – *Edward Poe*

MEET THE AUTHOR

———⊷⊷⊷———

Patrice S. Jordan is the President of Her Secret Vault/Bosses Build Business Credit. She is a well-known business credit expert, business consultant, and entrepreneur. With over ten years of entrepreneurial experience in many different areas of business, Patrice has become recognized as an authority in business credit building, acquiring business vehicles with no personal guarantee (PG), business consulting, and business credit scoring.

She has a passion for people and is dedicated to sharing her knowledge. Patrice is inspired by the community. She creates mentorship opportunities for those who need help in their business. These include building business credit, funding ideas, creating structure, gaining no PG vehicles, as well as so much more.

Her goal has always been to help people create multiple streams of income and provide them with a hub of knowledge. Patrice loves to better educate other business professionals because she believes everyone deserves to win.

1

THE PERFECT
BUSINESS STRUCTURE

T he first thing we are going to talk about is structuring your business. Now, you may be thinking: *Why are we starting here?* Well, I'm about to tell you exactly why.

You see, when it comes to building your business credit, all of the lenders you will be seeking to open business credit accounts with (banks, vendors, auto dealerships, corporate leasing companies, etc.) want to see that you have a legitimate business which is *structured and set up correctly*.

I want you to remember one thing as you start to learn and understand what I am sharing with you—and as you get deeper into this book—one of the key principles of business credit is not just *what* you get approved for, but also *how much* you get approved for. Before we move on, I want to emphasize: **It is important to master this section before doing/applying anything else in the rest of this book.**

I have carefully laid out this information in a specific order to teach you the fundamentals so that you can set up your business correctly.

In this book I am not only teaching you *what* to do and *how* to do it but also *when* to do it! This is why I received over 200 five-star reviews on Google in just nine months!

YOUR BUSINESS CREDIT PROFILE

When you are building business credit, vendors and creditors will use your business credit profile to determine the creditability and lending ability of your business. This profile includes detailed information about your business credit accounts, including utilities, credit cards, banks, suppliers, and other creditors.

This information will include the dates when your accounts were established, any current outstanding balances, any past due accounts, and a detailed history of all your payments. It also provides information available from public records about your business pulled from city, state, county, and federal records, including any potentially negative information about tax liens, lawsuits, judgments, and previous bankruptcy. All of this information informs the lender whether or not your business is credible.

Let's jump straight into understanding your credit profile breakdown.

Make Sure Your Profile is Accurate

It's not uncommon for business owners to find errors in their profiles. Fortunately, the business credit reporting bureaus (the three biggest are Dun & Bradstreet, Equifax, and Experian) are extremely motivated to make sure their data is accurate. Since they sell access to their information to lenders, inaccurate or out-of-date information isn't very valuable!

All three have processes in place to resolve legitimate disputes and correct verifiable errors. What's important to note is that sometimes even minor errors in your profile can make it more difficult for your business to qualify for a loan.

Keep your Personal and Business Credit Separate

This can sometimes be a challenge for business owners, particularly during the early years when business credit is harder to come by. Nevertheless, finding ways to establish business credit and avoiding the use of your personal credit is the best course of action.

For example, instead of using your personal credit cards to purchase supplies or pay for expenses related to your business, apply for a business card. Not only will this help you to establish business credit, but the higher balances that often accompany business expenses can actually hurt your personal credit score because 30 percent of that score is a reflection of how much credit you have, compared to how much credit you use. (This is true even if you pay the balance down to zero at the end of every payment cycle.)

Using your personal credit card does nothing to build a stronger business credit profile, and it will be harder to access business loans down the road. This route also protects you from being personally liable if your business is sued or takes on debt; it will all fall under the business.

Establish Trade Accounts With Your Suppliers

This is one of the best things you can do early in your business to build a strong credit foundation.

Make Sure Your Suppliers Report Your Good Credit Behavior

If your suppliers are not reporting your good history to the bureaus, you may be building a good credit reputation with that particular vendor, but you're not doing anything to build a good credit profile. This is important enough that you should ask every vendor you work with if they report to the credit bureaus; you need to seek out those that do.

Use the Credit You Need and Stay Current

The single biggest thing you can do to positively impact your business credit profile is to make regular and timely payments on your business credit accounts. Avoiding the use of credit entirely isn't a good long-term strategy because building a strong profile is about demonstrating that you know how to effectively leverage credit when you need it and that you will make periodic payments on time when you borrow.

WHAT YOU NEED IN PLACE TO START BUILDING A STRONG BUSINESS PROFILE

Business Address

Your business address can make or break your business! ABSOLUTELY DO NOT USE UPS or PO boxes. Get a virtual address instead. When picking a virtual address, STAY AWAY FROM COMPANIES LIKE IPOSTAL as they have 99.9 percent BAD addresses for businesses when it comes to building business credit.

Using these addresses will get your profile FLAGGED very quickly. If you've already set up your business with one of these addresses, there is a way to correct this. You will need to file an amendment with your Secretary of State and the IRS after you get a better location.

If you have an actual physical brick-and-mortar location, this also applies to you. Use your actual physical location and stay away from using your home address (it's public information and doesn't cut it when it comes to getting major funding). Below is a list of companies that you can choose from to obtain a good address. However, please conduct your own research by doing an online search of the address before locking it down, and make sure that it comes up as an office building. THIS IS VERY IMPORTANT!

- ➤ Virtual/Corporate Alliance
- ➤ Regus

> ➤ Opus (reports to the credit bureaus). They will also give you a business phone toll-free number. Click the link in my bio on IG (@hersesecretvault) to go directly to this company.

Business Phone Number

Once you have your address secured, you want to acquire a business toll-free phone number. Here are some options: Grasshopper, eVoice, or Opus.

For those of you who use your cell phone number as your business phone number, please know that your cell phone number is not the same as a business phone number. Your business needs to have a separate phone number. And while you may even have a separate local number for your business, it is best when building your business to have a toll-free number because it makes your business seem bigger than it is, giving it a "national presence."

Business Email

Having a professional email shows lenders that they can trust your business. In my professional experience, I have seen that they will oftentimes lend you more money just by having a real business email address. When building business credit, lenders and creditors want to see a real business email such as info@hersecretvault. net or orders@hersecretvault.net. Please DO NOT USE Gmail or Yahoo, etc. Some other options are: GoDaddy, Namecheap, or Google Workspace.

Set Up Your Business Legal Structure

Incorporate your business as a Limited Liability Company (LLC) or a Corporation with the Secretary of State (SOS) office. While there are companies that can do this for you, you can do this yourself by going to your state's SOS website and applying online or in person.

If you want to use a company to do this, I recommend Laughlin Associates who will report your payments to the credit bureaus. (If you decide to explore this option, ask for Wayne Schoenberger and please tell him Patrice S. Jordan from Her Secret Vault referred you.) His current contact information is:

Local:	775-883-8484
Toll-free:	800-648-0966
Email:	wschoenberger@laughlinUSA.com

Get Your Employee Identification Number (EIN)

You can apply for an EIN online at IRS.gov for FREE; however, be aware that there is another site that is copying the IRS and will ask you to pay. If you find yourself at this site asking for a payment, just refresh your browser and apply for your EIN FREE at the official IRS website.

Open a Business Bank Account

Open this right away even if you have no intentions of using it immediately. The older your business bank account is, the better it will be for you when applying for business credit. Some options

I suggest are: Navy Federal Credit Union, Wells Fargo, Bank of America, or any credit union.

Unique Entity Identifier (UEI)

The Unique Entity Identifier (UEI) is a required number for businesses and organizations seeking to apply for federal grants and contracts in the United States. It replaces the DUNS number and is used to uniquely identify entities in federal systems.

To apply for a UEI, follow these steps:

1. Visit the SAM.gov website: Go to [SAM.gov] (https://sam.gov), the official U.S. government system for managing federal grants and procurement.
2. Register your entity: Create an account and register your entity by providing required information such as your business details, Taxpayer Identification Number (TIN), and banking information.
3. Complete the application Follow the prompts to complete the application process. Ensure that all information provided is accurate and up to date.
4. Receive your UEI: Once your registration is processed, you will be issued a UEI which you can use for all federal grant and contract applications.

By obtaining a UEI, your organization will be eligible to participate in federal funding opportunities, facilitating growth and development through government support.

Feel free to adjust this to better fit the style and tone of your book!

Establish Your Online Presence

You need an online presence. THIS IS THE MEAT AND POTATOES of your profile! If a lender or vendor can't find you online, they WILL NOT lend to you.

Step 1: Set up a business website

Having a business website is very important to lenders and creditors. They want to see that you are real and have an online presence. This does not need to be a step to stress about. Even if you only have a one-page landing page, that is fine. If you want to build one yourself, some options I recommend are GoDaddy, Wix, or Squarespace.

Step 2: List your business on ListYourself.net

ListYourself.net is designed to help get your phone number listed in the 411 phone directory assistance. For millions of people, picking up a phone and calling directory assistance remains their preferred way to find and connect with others.

Establish Your Business Credit Profile With the Three Main Business Credit Agencies

1. **D&B**: Largest credit reporting agency. This is where you would generate a "Paydex" score. A score of 80–100 is "low risk" and where you want to be at all times. (Tip: Add three

net-30 vendors that report to DNB to acquire a score in 30 days.)

2. **Experian**: Second largest credit monitoring agency that's used by credit card companies to determine your approval. Make sure your business score is 76–100 before applying for credit cards.

3. **Equifax Commercial**: Third largest credit reporting agency. Most lenders pull from here when making lending decisions.

Monitor Your Business Credit Profiles

You can also monitor your business credit profile with all three of the main business credit agencies via Nav.com. However, please remember that Nav pulls from all three of the agencies and ONLY monitors your scores. This is not where your scores are generated.

One of the most powerful benefits of using Nav is that it can also be used as a tradeline (this is discussed more in chapter 4). Use the following link to get a discount on Nav: https://bit.ly/37qBuVh.

2

DIFFERENT TYPES OF LEGAL STRUCTURES FOR YOUR BUSINESS

In this chapter I am going to go through some of the most commonly used business structures. Some of them you may be familiar with and others you may not be! When setting up your business structure, it is important to take into consideration several different factors, such as the risk level of your business, your business goals and objectives, and also your personal goals and objectives.

I also strongly advise that you get professional advice to ensure that your business is legally structured in a way that is most appropriate for your circumstances.

Sole Proprietorship

A sole proprietorship is easy to form and gives you complete control of your business. You're automatically considered to be a sole proprietor if you perform business activities but don't register as any other kind of business. Sole proprietorships do not produce a separate business entity. This means your business assets and liabilities are not separate from your personal assets and liabilities, and you can be held personally liable for the debts and obligations of the business.

If you operate as a sole proprietor, you are still able to get a trade name, but it can also be harder to raise money because you can't sell stock, and banks are hesitant to lend to sole proprietorships.

Operating as a sole proprietor can be a good choice for low-risk businesses and owners who want to test their business idea before forming a more formal business.

Partnerships

Partnerships are the simplest structure for two or more people to own a business together. There are two common kinds of partnerships: limited partnership (LP) and limited liability partnership (LLP). Limited partnerships have only one general partner with unlimited liability, and all other partners have limited liability.

The partners with limited liability also tend to have limited control over the company, which is documented in a partnership agreement. Profits are passed through to personal tax returns, and the general partner—the partner without limited liability—must also pay self-employment taxes. LLPs are like limited partnerships but give limited liability to every owner. An LLP protects each partner from debts against the partnership, meaning they won't be responsible for the actions of other partners.

Partnerships can be a good choice for businesses with multiple owners, professional groups (like attorneys), and other groups that want to test their business idea before forming a more formal business.

Limited Liability Company (LLC)

An LLC is a form of business that lets you take advantage of the benefits of both the corporation and partnership business structures.

LLCs protect you from personal liability. In most instances, your personal assets, such as your vehicle, house, and savings accounts, won't be at risk in case your LLC faces bankruptcy or lawsuits. Profits and losses can get passed through to your personal income without facing corporate taxes. However, members of an LLC are considered self-employed and must pay self-employment tax contributions toward Medicare and Social Security. LLCs can have a limited life in many states.

When a member joins or leaves an LLC, some states may require the LLC to be dissolved and re-formed with new membership—unless there's already an agreement in place within the LLC for buying, selling, and transferring ownership.

LLCs can be a good choice for medium- or higher-risk businesses, owners who have significant personal assets they want to be protected, and owners who want to pay a lower tax rate than they would with a corporation.

C Corporation (C Corp)

A C corporation, sometimes called a C corp, is a legal entity that's separate from its owners. Corporations can make a profit, can be taxed, and can be held legally liable.

Corporations offer the strongest protection to their owners from personal liability, but the cost to form a corporation is higher than other structures. Corporations also require more extensive record keeping, operational processes, and reporting.

Unlike sole proprietors, partnerships, and LLCs, corporations pay income tax on their profits. In some cases, corporate profits are taxed twice: first, when the company makes a profit, and again when dividends are paid to shareholders on their personal tax returns.

Corporations have a completely independent life separate from their shareholders. If a shareholder leaves the company or sells his or her shares, the C corp can continue doing business relatively undisturbed.

Corporations have an advantage when it comes to raising capital because they can raise funds through the sale of stock, which can also be a benefit in attracting employees. Corporations can be a good choice for medium- or higher-risk businesses, businesses that need to raise money, and businesses that plan to "go public" or eventually be sold.

S Corp

An S corporation, sometimes called an S corp, is a special type of corporation that's designed to avoid the double taxation drawback of regular C corps. S corps allow profits, and some losses, to be passed through directly to owners' personal income without ever being subject to corporate tax rates.

Not all states tax S corps equally, but most recognize them the same way the federal government does and taxes the shareholders accordingly. Some states tax S corps on profits above a specified limit, and other states don't recognize the S corp election at all, simply treating the business as a C corp. S corps must file with the IRS to get S corp status, a different process from registering with their state.

There are special limits on S corps. S corps can't have more than 100 shareholders, and all shareholders must be U.S. citizens. If you operate as an S corp, you'll still have to follow the strict filing and operational processes of a C corp. S corps also have an independent life, just like C corps. If a shareholder leaves the company or sells his or her shares, the S corp can continue doing business relatively undisturbed.

S corps can be a good choice for businesses that would otherwise be a C corp but meet the criteria to file as an S corp.

B Corp

A benefit corporation, sometimes called a B corp, is a for-profit corporation recognized by a majority of U.S. states. B corps are different from C corps in purpose, accountability, and transparency but aren't different in how they're taxed. B corps are driven by both mission and profit. Shareholders hold the company accountable to produce some sort of public benefit in addition to a financial profit.

Some states require B corps to submit annual benefit reports that demonstrate their contribution to the public good. There are several third-party B corp certification services, but none are required for a company to be legally considered a B corp in a state where the legal status is available.

Close Corporation

Close corporations resemble B corps but have a less traditional corporate structure. These shed many formalities that typically govern corporations and apply to smaller companies. State rules vary, but shares are usually barred from public trading. Close corporations can be run by a small group of shareholders without a board of directors.

Nonprofit Corporation

Nonprofit corporations are organized to do charity, education, religious, literary, or scientific work. Because their work benefits the public, nonprofits can receive tax-exempt status, meaning they don't pay state or federal taxes or income taxes on any profits they make. Nonprofits must file with the IRS to get tax exemption, a different process from registering with their state. Nonprofit corporations need to follow organizational rules very similar to a regular C corp. They also need to follow special rules about what they do with any profits they earn. For example, they can't distribute profits to members or political campaigns.

Nonprofits are often called 501(c)(3) corporations—a reference to the section of the Internal Revenue Code that is most commonly used to grant tax-exempt status.

Cooperative

A cooperative is a business or organization owned by and operated for the benefit of those using its services. Profits and earnings generated by the cooperative are distributed among the members, also known as user-owners.

Typically, an elected board of directors and officers runs the cooperative while regular members have voting power to control the direction of the cooperative. Members can become part of the cooperative by purchasing shares, though the number of shares they hold does not affect the weight of their vote.

COMBINING DIFFERENT BUSINESS STRUCTURES

Designations like S corp and nonprofit aren't strictly business structures—they can also be understood as a tax status. It's possible for an LLC to be taxed as a C corp, an S corp, or a nonprofit. These arrangements are far less common and can be more difficult to set up.

If you're considering one of these non-standard structures, you should speak with a business counselor or an attorney to help you decide which structure and tax status is most appropriate for you and your business.

3

WHAT EIN-ONLY BUSINESS CREDIT REALLY IS

I n this chapter I want to take a moment to explain to you what EIN-only business credit really means. EIN-only business credit is the ability for a/your business to operate/stand alone on its own.

Think of EIN-only business credit the same way you would think about you having a social security number. As an individual person, you are identified by the government, credit bureaus, and many others by your social security number.

In order for you to purchase a house, buy a car, get a cell phone, buy land, etc., you need to have good personal credit. Your social security number and you are one person.

With your business, it is no different. You need to build a strong business credit profile in stages for your business to be able to stand alone by itself so that you don't have to act as a personal guarantor for your business.

To do this, you will need to build business credit from tier 1 through tier 5 without skipping steps. Doing this will give your business the ability to build a strong foundation for itself and therefore put it in a position to stand alone without attaching your personal social security number (unless it's for identification purposes only).

Before we move on to the next chapter, I want you to be very clear about what this means. Before providing your social security number to ANY vendor, make sure they are just trying to confirm that you are a real person and they are not "PGing" (personal guaranteeing) you.

Just to be safe, I suggest that you immediately lock all of your personal credit accounts with the three major credit bureaus. This can be done by calling them or notifying them online.

chapter

4

BUILDING BUSINESS CREDIT (EIN ONLY)

As we just discussed in chapter 3, when it comes to building business credit without using your social security number as a personal guarantee, you have to create a profile where the business can stand alone.

To accomplish this, you need to look at the five associated tiers. When you consider these tiers, think of MAJOR vendors, i.e., vendors that are everywhere.

While you are building your business credit profile, do not apply for major vendors out of the proper tier. While building, I want you to focus not on just what you get approved for but how much.

When you apply in the correct tier, your approval amounts will be MUCH higher. You should expect nothing under $10K per approval.

Now we get to work! As you read this chapter, I want you to keep two things in mind:

1. FOLLOW EACH STEP **IN ORDER.** DO NOT SKIP ANY STEPS, PLEASE.
2. RUN YOUR OWN RACE AND STAY FOCUSED ON YOUR BUSINESS PROFILE!

BUILDING TIER 1: NET-30/ Subscription Vendors

Opening accounts with net-30/subscription vendors will help you get started with building tier 1 business credit. Below is a list of vendors that can help you establish your business credit; you need to use these vendors until they report. If done right, they can report within forty-five to sixty days or less. When it comes to the net-30 vendors accounts, DO NOT PAY ON THE EXACT DATE THAT YOUR INVOICES ARE DUE. Pay about two weeks after your purchase to acquire a higher Paydex score! For the subscription-based vendors, you keep them until they report to the Business bureau. Then you can stop your subscription. And, no, they won't take your score away from you after they report. The goal here is to apply and get approved for these credit accounts. Make sure you have at least three vendors that report to DNB to gain a Paydex score. I always recommend getting four to five accounts right away, as out of the five, three will report faster. Here are my recommendations: Quill; Grainger; Uline; Nav ($39.99); eCredable ($19.99).

Order from Grainger, Uline, and Quill between $100 and $200 per month. The more you spend, the better your results. Order on Thursdays and then pay your invoices the second or third Monday after your purchase. This shows the vendors that you're responsible.

Nav.com tracks your business profile and has every type of business service you will need as a business owner. A great benefit of enrolling with Nav is that if you upgrade your Nav account to the credit builder ($39.99 or higher at the time of this publication), it will report your monthly payment to all three credit agencies. In other words, this will be adding a new tradeline to your profile, which I highly recommend.

Keep in mind that NAV stands for the net asset value of your company, nothing more nothing less. After the tradeline reports, you can stop paying for it. Once you stop paying, you will then see a letter score, not a number. PLEASE don't freak out. Nav is only a tradeline. The bureaus are the ones that generate your credit score; Nav merely monitors it.

Credit ratings are normally expressed in letters such as "A" or "B". A and B letters are good. Just a quick FYI on your Nav profile— You may see a low Equifax score. No worries, as Equifax comes into play more around tier 3. And by the time you get to tier 3, you would see a better Equifax score. Equifax is always the last score to go up as there are only certain vendors that only report to them.

eCredable Lift offers a way to potentially improve your credit score by reporting your utility, cell phone, and internet payment history to credit bureaus. Here are the key features and benefits of the service:

1. Utility and Telecom Payments Reporting: By reporting up to twenty-four months of your utility, cell phone, and internet payment history, eCredable Lift can help you build or improve your credit profile. This can be particularly

beneficial if you have a limited credit history or are trying to rebuild your credit.

2. Improved Credit Opportunities: With an improved credit score, you may qualify for better credit cards and personal loans, potentially saving money through lower interest rates and better terms.

3. Monthly Credit Score Updates eCredable Lift provides monthly updates of your VantageScore 3.0 credit score, allowing you to monitor your progress and see the impact of the reported payments over time.

This service can be especially useful for individuals who have a thin credit file or no traditional credit history, enabling them to leverage their consistent payment habits to build a stronger credit profile.

NET 30 MEANS BUY NOW, PAY LATER. As for Nav, as long as you have the $39.99-and-above package, they will report to the bureaus on your business's behalf. Please note that 99.9 percent of net-30 vendors don't ask for EIN. They report to DNB based on your business information, so make sure it matches up.

BUILDING TIER 2: RETAIL CARDS

All three vendors from tier 1 should be reporting to DNB before moving onto tier 2. Remember, when applying for business retail, do not put your social security number on the application. If you are asked for this information, just leave it blank. This will force the company to pull your business credit. As with tier 1, the goal here is to apply and get approved for at least three of these retail cards. While having all of them is not mandatory, I do recommend and suggest that you apply for all: Staples; Home Depot; Lowes; Floor & Decor; NTB (National Tire & Battery).

BUILDING TIER 3: FLEET CREDIT TIER

All six combined vendors from tier 1 and tier 2 need to be reporting before moving onto this tier. Also, remember that when you apply for a business fleet, do not put your social security number on the application. Leave it blank!

Here are my recommendations: Shell gas card, BP Master Card, and Chevron gas card.

BUILDING TIER 4: MAJOR CREDIT CARD

Make sure your Experian score is between 78 and 100 before applying for credit cards. And, remember, when applying for business credit cards, do not put your social security number on the application. Leave it blank. This will force the company to pull your business credit.

Now, when applying, if you get a message saying that your EIN and social security number can't be the same, call the vendor instead and apply online, letting them know you don't want to personally guarantee "PG" this application: Sam's Club Master Card; Amazon Net 55; Wells Fargo; Capital One.

BUILDING TIER 5: BUSINESS LOANS

When you get to this stage, congratulate yourself! You have entered the BIG, BIG LEAGUES now! Now, before getting funding in this tier, your Equifax score needs to be strong.

IMPORTANCE OF BUILDING TIERS IN ORDER

You already know by now: Do not apply for major vendors out of the proper tier because it's not what you get approved for but how much. And by applying in the correct tier, your approval amounts will be MUCH higher (nothing under $10K per approval). But before we wrap up and move on, I want to dive in a little deeper here. The tier 1 to tier 5 vendors listed in this chapter are considered major players in the business credit industry, but there are other vendors that you can apply for without skipping the major steps without getting declined.

What follows is a better explanation:

BP gas (major) tier 3; Arco gas (not major); you can apply in tier 1.

Staples (major) tier 2: Business T-Shirt Club (not major) tier 1.

Capital One (major) tier 4; BILL Spend & Expense (not major) tier 1 (with income to show).

Note: If you run into any issues with acquiring your tier 1 vendors, here is a script below to help you.

Calling Vendors (this script works better with Quill):

Once a representative answers, they are going to introduce themselves and then ask you for your name.

You: "Hello my name is _____. I would like to speak to an account manager/supervisor please."

(The representative is going to seem kind of confused when you ask for an account manager and will then start to ask you questions.)

You: Make it seem like you're very disappointed with their customer service from the other representatives. Tell the representative that you were placed on hold for about thirty minutes and that the phone/representative then hung up on you before coming back to the phone to address your issues fully. The representative will apologize and try to help.

You will then let the representative know you were advised that if you placed an order, your account would be a net 30. Tell them you are disappointed that the previous representative lied to you and then hung up on you.

The representative will then place you on hold and try to contact their supervisor. If they don't place you on hold, they will probably try to help you themselves.

If the representative comes back and says that you have to place five to seven orders before they can grant you net 30, you have to stick to the script and say, "I need to speak to your supervisor; this is unacceptable. If I knew that you wanted me to submit five to seven orders in advance, I would have never opened this account. I am not responsible for the misinformation provided by your team member who is supposed to be trained and knowledgeable in customer service (and might I add was very rude)."

The representative will then tell you that you have to, at least, place an order.

Option 1: If you placed an order before, advise the representative that you placed an order and the account is still not a net 30. Then use that against the representative by saying, "You are telling me the same thing, but, as you can see, my account is not a net 30." At that point, the representative should have someone update your account to net 30.

Option 2: Advise the representative that you have an existing order sitting in your cart. Tell them, "I don't mind submitting that order as long as my account will be marked as net 30." (Have $100 worth of items in your cart.)

Option 3: If the representative starts to piss you off, hang up and take a deep breath. Call them again and inform them that you were hung up on (LOL!).

The reason for net 30 and going so hard is you can buy now and pay later, which is a win-win!

You will also find on YouTube a training video for those of you who learn better by watching video steps:

https://www.youtube.com/watch?v=gk4QGLEnjjM

5

PURCHASE/
LEASE A VEHICLE

The key here is: STRUCTURE, STRUCTURE, STRUCTURE. Go back to the beginning of the book and reread if necessary. When it comes to getting a vehicle under your business, MOST dealership salespeople will have no idea what you are talking about. You are about to find yourself in the position of educating the dealership's salesperson, and NO professional wants to be told how to do their JOB. Always ask to speak with the finance manager so you can explain to them who you are and what you're wanting to accomplish (purchase a vehicle under your business with no money down). Tell them that you would like an application to be sent to you via email.

Don't waste your time going to the dealership. Even if they invite you in to the dealership, say that you are not available—unless you want to spend hours in the dealership getting the runaround!

If a dealership tells you that they don't do any applications without PG, that's because they are trying to run your application with their in-house company. That's not what you need. You to want to finance with ALLY ONLY. Ally doesn't require ANY DOCUMENTS from you, not even an income statement. If your business is making income and you want to go with their in-house company, you can just make sure they tell them you are not looking to PG and you are not putting any money down.

Keep in mind that, after submitting your application, you will experience all sorts of deception from the dealership, especially when they think you are trying to educate them. Here are some key things they love to tell you:

We submitted your application and it was declined. (Nope, they never submitted it.)

We submitted your application, and you were approved but they are asking for PG. (NOPE.)

We submitted your application, and you were approved but they are asking for money down. (NOPE.)

We submitted your application, and you were declined due to insufficient credit. (NOPE.)

We submitted your application, and you were DECLINED because your business is new. (NOPE.)

These are all stall tactics by the dealership because you challenged them!

Say thank you and move on to the next one. You may have to go through three to five declines before you get that one yes, but when you do, it's all uphill from there. Once you are approved, you have thirty days from the purchase of the first vehicle to get as many cars as possible from the dealership before they report on your profile. Once one purchased car is reported, your score will drop if you don't have tidelines to offset the loan of the car.

Some places may also tell you that you can't get approved for another vehicle for several months. *Go to another dealership* and run the play all over again. Don't take no for an answer. The dealership may even tell you that Ally will only finance one vehicle, so they can't finance another one. This is not true—just keep going! Note: Stay away from mom and pop dealers. They are harder to get corporate leases from UNLESS you're buying WITH CASH.

Recommended Dealers:

Mercedes-Benz of Myrtle Beach, South Carolina; Lexus dealerships; Mercedes-Benz dealership; Kia dealership; Dodge Chrysler; Jeep Ram; GMC.

It's best to pick the make and model of the vehicle you want ahead of time. You can then either call the dealer and talk to the commercial finance manager or visit the dealership.

Ask questions about your vehicle choice and options for putting it under your business. Bonus tip: You can refinance your personal vehicle under your business.

Bring all of your business documents. They don't need them, but it's best to cover yourself. Ask for the fleet manager. Be upfront about what your purpose is. DO NOT: PG.

Be okay with saying no and moving onto another dealership if they seem confused or insist that you PG.

LET YOUR CARS PAY FOR THEMSELVES!

List it on Turo:

What is Turo and how does it work? Turo is a car-sharing platform similar to Airbnb. As a corporate vehicle owner, you can list your cars on Turo as often as you want each month. The money made should be used to pay your insurance and car note. The additional money made after paying your car note and insurance is profit in your pocket. The rest of the month you can do as you please with your luxury vehicle. (Tip: this is a six-figure business idea).

Check Turo in your area first to see what cars are listed and how they are performing in the market before choosing a car to list. This platform works just as well for cars sitting in your driveway. Put your vehicles to use! Stop sitting on them, and make sure to take clear photos of your vehicle.

1You will need a valid driver's license, VIN #, the exact address of the car's location, and a license plate. Have clear photos of the entire car. Have a minimum trip duration (start with one day to test the waters). Turn "advance notice" on. List your cars, and make those listing sounds like someone's dream car (use your own words).

Note: If a guest contacts you for early check-ins, advise them to do it through Turo. This protects you because Turo insurance doesn't kick in until the actual time for the check-in.

Maintenance Check:

Horn works; mirrors work; brakes work; engine starts; seat belts work; trunk works; the body of the vehicle has no scratches or damage; lights work; turn signals work; under your hood is good!

Always fuel your vehicles and have a lockbox just in case you're not able to be there for the physical check-in. Recommendation: Yourmechanic.com (they will come to you).

Check-In:

Make sure your guest has all of their documents uploaded before coming to pick up the vehicle. Upon arrival, check your guest's ID and make sure that it's valid.

Tip: A little hack that you can use is to download an app called Bar & Club Stats ID scanner. You can scan their ID to make sure it's real.

Do a full walk around the car with the guest and take pictures, upload the photos into Turo yourself (Do the same for checkouts when the guest returns the vehicle.)

Sometimes guests may want an extended day or hour. If so, have them extend via Turo. Remember to always protect your investments.

Protect Your Investment:

Always have commercial insurance (Liberty Mutual or State Farm are options). If you get into an accident, and you have regular insurance on a commercial vehicle, you will not be sitting in a good position at all. (Protect your investment.) If your guest gets a ticket, contact Turo so they can shift liability. In the event of an accident, report it within twenty-four hours to Turo. Put a GPS TRACKER on your vehicle, as some people will try to steal it (passtimegps. com), or try Bouncie with OBD plugin. Turo has something called

All-Star Host which provides you with bonuses and badges for good listings.

Tax Write-Off Bonus:

Vehicles under your business name can be written off (let's get educated). Read up on Section 179 of the U.S. federal tax code for additional breakdowns. Purchase and place your vehicles in service before the end of the year because the bigger the vehicle, the better the write-off.

No Limit Vehicles: You can write off the entire truck! Old or new, Sprinter vans, pickup trucks with a cargo bed, delivery vehicles, etc. There can be no business loss to claim this deduction; your business should show a profit at the end of the year.

BONUS: Lock and freeze your personal credit before heading down to the dealership. They are slick. Remember the goal is to build business credit under your EIN, not your social security number.

ADDITIONAL PLATFORMS TO LIST YOUR VEHICLES ON

Hyre Car:

- ➤ Insurance: included
- ➤ Compensation: You will get 75% of your earnings
- ➤ 25% fee
- ➤ Partners with Uber and Lyft, offering drivers to rent your car to drive for ridesharing apps.

Getaround:

- ➤ 0% fee to use platform.
- ➤ Users can unlock your vehicle with a digital key that's available in the Getaround app for iPhone and Android. So there's no need to meet them to exchange keys.
- ➤ Insurance: trips are covered by a $1M insurance policy.
- ➤ Compensation: You will receive your compensation— 60% of your bookings—by check or via PayPal.

Pick up Scooters:

This is a good options to get your kids involved in the business. If you have a larger vehicle, such as a pickup truck, you could partner with Lime to pick up their scooters.

Your responsibility as a Lime Juicer is to pick up Lime scooters from the street for a charge. You should also return the scooters back to the streets when they are fully charged. You could make on average $8 per scooter and get paid weekly.

Help Move Houses (Dolly)

If you own a larger vehicle, like a pickup truck or a truck, you can earn money helping people move between houses.

Dolly is an online platform connecting you with people who are seeking people with trucks to help them move. As a Dolly helper, you'll typically get gigs to move furniture or large home appliances. You can expect to make $30/hour delivering or moving things with Dolly. Dolly typically issues payment to helpers on Fridays for previous week's work via PayPal.

Carpooling (Lyft)

Provide Transportation for Children (Hop Skip Drive)

BEST COMMERCIAL VEHICLE INSURANCE

ABI Web Insurance

Now, let me be clear. Even though ABI is the best insurance for commercial vehicles, it gets us flagged at some dealerships because it's super cheap. To avoid any unnecessary confusion or delays, I would suggest getting some other insurance just to furnish to the dealership. Once you have been approved and you drive off, then you can cancel whatever insurance you got and sign up for ABI or have ABI set up already so you have no lapse in your insurance.

DISPOSING OF YOUR CAR LEASE

Swap A Lease: Easy car lease

My Car Option: The easiest way to sell your car for the most money

Lease Tracker: Transfer your lease

Quit A Lease: The most reliable name in car leasing

6

HOW TO START A
GAS CARD RENTAL BUSINESS

Now that you have started your own trucking or car rental business, you are simply not going to utilize all of the money by yourself. I recommend that you connect with other people in this community or Facebook and offer your gas cards to them to rent out.

Gas cards companies allow you to have multiple cards. Set a limit on the cards for all your new customers who will be renting from you. Always take a deposit of at least $500– $1,000 so that in the event one of the companies/customers defaults on their payment, you are not stuck. You also have the ability, at any point in time, to cut off their card (this is business not personal).

To find customers, go to Facebook and type in any industry you can think of that uses lots of gas: trucking groups, Turo rental groups, car rental groups, box truck groups, queen of trucking, etc.

Be sure to check in with the admins of these groups/communities first to post in the group. Some groups have a strict "no soliciting" policy, and they will block you immediately for posting. Also, have a simple contract to put in place, detailing what the customer/company is responsible for. You can have them use Zelle, a cash app, or you can invoice them every month via your processing company.

chapter

7

DEALERSHIP LIST

If you own a business, you should know the tax rules for buying an SUV or a truck. You can and should deduct the operating expense of your vehicle if you use it for your business. But you can also deduct the cost of your SUV or truck as well. With the tax reform act passed at the end of 2017, buying a truck or an SUV that is over 6,000 pounds has become more favorable for 2018 and beyond. Here are the tax deduction rules for SUVs and trucks.

Tax Deduction Rule

You can only write off 100% if the vehicle is used 100% for business AND you buy it brand new from the dealer (no private party used vehicle). It has to be brand new. The amount in the example factors in a brand new SUV over 6,000 pounds.

To summarize:

1. If an asset is used 100% for business purposes, the entire amount is deductible. Otherwise, the deductible amount corresponds to the percentage of business use. For example, if an asset is used 65% for business, then 65% of its depreciation or other deductions can be claimed. Keep a mileage log! It's generally impossible to have 100% business use, hence the more conservative 95% depreciation used in the above example.

2. Must be a brand new SUV over 6,000 lbs. The IRS allows up to $25K upfront depreciation (100%) for SUVs over 6,000 pounds. PLUS, 50% bonus depreciation for NEW vehicles which will get close to that figure. The vehicle must be driven over 50% of the miles for business purposes. Further, you must reduce the $25K by the personal use percentage.

What vehicle can you write off fully? The maximum first-year depreciation write-off is $11,200, plus up to an additional $8,000 in bonus depreciation. For SUVs with loaded vehicles of weights over 6,000 pounds, but no more than 14,000 pounds, 100% of the cost can be expensed using bonus depreciation in 2023.

Trucks, vans, and sport utility vehicles as defined in the Internal Revenue Code with a GVWR over 6,000 pounds and placed in service during 2023 qualify for immediate depreciation deductions of up to 100% of the purchase price.

2023 List of vehicles that qualify for Section 179:

- Audi Q7
- BMW X5, X6
- Buick Enclave
- Cadillac XT5, XT6, Escalade
- Chevrolet Silverado, Suburban, Tahoe
- Traverse
- Chrysler Pacifica
- Dodge Durango, Grand Caravan
- Ford Expedition, Explorer, F-150 and larger
- GMC Acadia, Sierra, Yukon
- Honda Pilot 4WD, Odyssey
- Infiniti QX80, QX56
- Jeep Grand Cherokee
- Land Rover Range Rover, Discovery
- Lexus GX460, LX570
- Lincoln MKT AWD, Navigator
- Mercedes-Benz G550, GLS, GLE, Metris
- Sprinter
- Nissan Armada, NV 1500, NVP 3500, Titan
- Porsche Cayenne
- Tesla Model X
- Toyota 4Runner, Land Cruiser, Sequoia
- Tundra

BEFORE CONTACTING ANY OF THESE DEALERSHIPS, READ THE NEXT LINE TWICE.

THIS IS A LIST OF DEALERSHIPS THAT MY STUDENTS HAVE GOTTEN APPROVED FROM FOR $0 DOWN AND ZERO PG.

NEVER GO TO THE DEALERSHIP AND REVEAL YOUR HAND. WE KNOW ABOUT THEM, BUT THEY DON'T NEED TO KNOW ABOUT US. DON'T WALK INTO THE DEALERSHIP AND SAY THINGS LIKE: SOMEONE I KNOW OR SOMEONE IN HER SECRET VAULT COMMUNITY SENT ME HERE.

AGAIN, KEEP IN MIND THE DEALERSHIP PLAYS A HECK OF A LOT OF GAMES WITH US. NOW IT'S OUR TIME TO RETURN THE FAVOR (LOL).

STEP 1: FIND THE VEHICLE YOU WANT FIRST.

STEP 2: Contact them via phone and ASK for a business application via email. NO, YOU CAN'T GO IN FOR A TEST DRIVE. YOU'RE BUSY.

STEP 3: NEVER complete the personal information section with your personal information. Most dealerships don't have two separate applications, so they will send a personal application. That's fine. Complete it with all of your business information only.

STEP 4: Be sure that all communication is handled via your business email ONLY.

STEP 5: BEWARE OF THESE STRATEGIES THE DEALERSHIP MAY USE TO DETER YOU:

A. YOU DON'T HAVE ENOUGH BUSINESS CREDIT (BS)
B. YOUR BUSINESS IS TOO NEW (BS)
C. MOST LENDERS REQUIRE 20% DOWN (BS)

D. THEY WILL CONSIDER THE LOAN WITH A PERSONAL GUARANTEE (MAJOR BS. ONCE THEY GET AHOLD OF YOUR SOCIAL SECURITY NUMBER, IT'S A WRAP FOR YOUR CREDIT)

HERE IS A LIST OF DEALERSHIPS SOME OF MY STUDENTS GOT APPROVED AT. KEEP IN MIND YOU DON'T HAVE TO BE LIVING IN THAT STATE TO GET A VEHICLE FROM THAT DEALERSHIP.

- The Motor Mall, Macomb, MI
- Towbin Motors, Las Vegas, NV
- Jim Riehl's Friendly Chrysler Jeep, Sterling
- Heights, MI
- Crest Ford, Sterling Heights, MI
- Bill Snethkamp, Highland Park, MI
- Mercedes-Benz, Rochester Hills, MI
- Darcars Toyota, Silver Springs, MD
- Rockwall Chrysler Dodge, TX
- La Riche Chevrolet Cadillac, MI
- Don Davis, Arlington, TX
- Mercedes-Benz, CA
- Gwinnett Chrysler Dodge Jeep, Stone Mountain, GA
- Monrovia CDJR, Monrovia, CA
- BMW, Grapevine, TX
- Audi, Grapevine, TX
- BMW, Plano, TX
- DFW Auto, Fort Worth, TX
- Helfman Dodge, Houston, TX

- DeMontrond Kia, Houston, TX
- Lou LaRiche, Plymouth, MI

WHAT FOLLOWS IS A LIST OF DEALERSHIPS SOME OF MY STUDENTS GOT APPROVED AT. KEEP IN MIND YOU DON'T HAVE TO BE LIVING IN THAT STATE TO GET A VEHICLE FROM THAT DEALERSHIP.

- Mercedes-Benz, Foothill, CA
- Mercedes-Benz, Ontario, CA
- Penske Cadillac Buick GMC of South Bay, Torrance, CA
- Southern States Hyundai, Raleigh, NC
- Vaden Nissan, Savannah, GA
- Toyota Chatham Parkway, Savannah, GA
- Murfreesboro Nissan, Nashville, TN
- Mercedes-Benz of Manhattan, New York, NY
- Off Lease Only, Orlando, FL
- Porsche of Farmington Hills, MI
- Napleton Chrysler Jeep Dodge, Kissimmee, FL
- Nissan of Murfreesboro, Murfreesboro, TN
- AutoNation, Miami, FL

chapter

8

LIST OF
RECOMMENDED
NO PG BANKS

Ally (Best Bank For Applying For Vehicles)
Other options:

➢ **Citizen Bank**
➢ **BMW Bank**
➢ **Ford Finance** (The dealership has the ability with almost
   every one of their finance companies to run your application without adding a PG, but you're going to have to
   educate them.)

chapter

9

DEALING WITH
THE DEALERSHIP

- ➢ Find the vehicle you want from the dealership.
- ➢ Contact the dealership via phone and ask for a business application to be sent via your business email.
- ➢ Send the application back with a copy of your driver's license.
- ➢ If asked for your social security number for identification purposes, DO NOT PROVIDE IT. Let them know your social security number is not a form of identification for your business.
- ➢ If the dealership comes back with a denial, move on to another dealership and follow the same instructions.

"Fail" reasons the dealership will give you:

- ➢ **Will consider with a PG.**

- ➤ The credit profile is not strong enough.
- ➤ Your business profile is too new.

You may get three to four denials before you get your first yes, as the dealership never wants to be proven wrong.

chapter

10

THE END/
YOUR NEW BEGINNING

N ow that we have come to the end of this book, it is really the beginning for you. It is my sincere desire that you will use the information I have given you in this book. Please use it to build your business credit, and, more importantly, to create your own lifestyle!

Before we wrap up, I want to leave you with one last secret, as well as share with you how you can manufacture spending.

One of the best and easiest ways to do this is through Stripe. To execute this, all you need to do is:

- ➤ Set up an account
- ➤ Invoice yourself
- ➤ Swipe your business credit card
- ➤ Use the funds to pay off any of your other cards
- ➤ And repeat!

49

This can also be done via PayPal or any merchant account. This process is also known, behind the scenes in the business world, as liquidating your credit card. The benefit of this process is that you can keep your rewards and utilize your business credit cards to help you build business credit.

Be sure to join Bosses Build Business Credit Group on Facebook if you're confused about anything laid out in this book. And always remember...

BOSSES BUILD BUSINESS CREDIT!

BONUS

**Fifteen Verified Easy Approval
Net-30 Accounts and Vendors**

1. The CEO Creative

The CEO Creative specializes in custom design and branding services but also carries products like electronics, office supplies, and apparel.

This makes their net-30 program a practical choice for many small business owners who are looking for affordable branding while simultaneously building business credit and boosting cash flow.

To qualify, you need to be a US-based business, have existed for at least thirty days, have a clean business credit history, and not have any late payment history.

Minimum orders needed to report to the credit bureau: $0

Membership fee per year: $49 to maintain net-30 account credit terms. Like most net-30 accounts, there are no interest rate charges.

Credit bureaus where transactions are reported:

- Dun & Bradstreet
- Equifax Business
- Creditsafe

Beneficial for businesses in these industries:

- B2B
- Medical
- Construction
- Manufacturing
- Restaurant supplies

2. JJ Gold International

Though JJ Gold International's product line of gift sets, decor products, jewelry, men's products, and eyewear won't apply to all businesses, their net-30 account bears mentioning.

They offer over 1,000 products and report to D&B and Experian Business, which can be instrumental in improving your business credit score while boosting cash flow.

To qualify for 30-day payment terms, you just need to be a US-based business, have operated for at least 30 days, and have a clean payment history with no late payments. Just note that JJ Gold International only offers net-30 terms on 50% of orders, and the other 50% must be paid upfront.

Minimum orders needed to report to the credit bureau: $100

Membership fee per year: $99 to maintain net-30 account payment terms

Credit bureaus where transactions are reported:

- Dun & Bradstreet
- Experian Business

Beneficial for businesses in these industries:

- Startups
- E-commerce businesses

3. Shogun Roasting

The new "no fee" net-30 account. Shogun Roasting is an exceptional coffee roasting company that has captured the hearts and palates of coffee enthusiasts around the globe. With a relentless dedication to quality and a deep respect for the art of roasting, Shogun Roasting has become synonymous with excellence in the coffee industry.

Minimum orders needed to report to the credit bureau: After one prepaid order you can apply for a business account

- For transactions to be reported, your account must contain a balance at the end of the month. Note that credit card purchases and same-month payments are not reported.

Membership fee per year: $0 to maintain net-30 account credit terms

Credit bureaus where transactions are reported:

- Experian
- Dun & Bradstreet
- Equifax
- Credit Safe

Beneficial for businesses in these industries:

- Home office
- Hospitality
- Healthcare
- Under ten employees

4. Wise Business Plans

Wise Business Plans provides various services relating to business plans and formations, business website design, business license searches, branding, digital marketing, business compliance, and others.

Businesses that want to apply for a net-30 credit line with Wise Business Plans must have a valid tax ID number or Employer Identification Number, be filed with the Secretary of State, and have no major business delinquencies. Applications are reviewed within 24 business hours, at which point the account will receive an initial credit limit.

Businesses that have qualified for a net-30 account will receive an approval email. The starter credit limit can grow over time if you have regular transactions with Wise Business Plans and make on-time payments. Additionally, net-30 accounts are reported monthly to credit bureaus. (See our Wise Business Plans Net-30 Review article for more details.)

Minimum orders needed to report to the credit bureau: $97

Membership fee per year: $99 to maintain net-30 account credit terms

Credit bureaus where transactions are reported:

- Experian
- Equifax
- Dun & Bradstreet
- Creditsafe

Beneficial for businesses in these industries:

- Local businesses
- Startups
- Franchises
- E-commerce businesses

5. NAMYNOT

As a digital marketing services firm, NAMYNOT offers a variety of online business marketing solutions such as SEO, social media marketing, content marketing, inbound lead generation, video production, and more.

Aside from having an Employer Identification Number, businesses that want to apply for a net-30 account with NAMYNOT must be established for at least 90 days, have a clean credit history, be registered in their respective states with good standing, and have a professional website, not a "Coming Soon" one.

NAMYNOT also offers credit lines that can go up to $10,000, and the approval process can take five to 10 business days.

Minimum orders needed to report to the credit bureau: $0

Membership fee per year: $0 to maintain net-30 account credit terms

Credit bureau where transactions are reported:

- Dun & Bradstreet

Beneficial for businesses in these industries:

- Telcos
- Online businesses or e-commerce shops
- Boutiques
- Tech companies or startups

6. Business T-Shirt Club

Unlike other companies selling apparel, the Business T-Shirt Club is exclusively for business owners and entrepreneurs. The company is membership-based wherein members can have access to high-quality apparel brands at wholesale rates. You will only be charged for custom print design and services.

Accounts that are approved for a net-30 billing will have their activities with Business T-Shirt Club reported every month.

Minimum orders needed to report to the credit bureau: 50% deposit on all orders for new members, which will be lifted after a minimum of five orders with no late or outstanding balances

Membership fee per year: $89.99 to maintain net-30 account credit terms

Credit bureaus where transactions are reported:

- Cortera
- Ansonia
- Equifax
- Experian
- Dun & Bradstreet
- Creditsafe

Beneficial for businesses in these industries:

- Retail businesses
- Hospitality
- Companies with field representatives

7. Creative Analytics

Focusing on growth marketing, web design, branding, and automation, Creative Analytics has a lot to offer B2B companies.

With nearly 20 years of experience and after serving over 22,000 clients, this net-30 vendor has a proven track record and strives to "captivate, convince, and convert audiences."

Note that this vendor has two net-30 account options for building business credit. You can pay $79 annually for an initial credit limit of $1,000. Or you can pay $49–$149 per month for an initial credit limit of $12,000.

To qualify for net-30 payment terms, you must be US-based, have been in business for at least 30 days, and not have any derogatory payment remarks.

Minimum orders needed to report to the credit bureaus: $100

Membership fee per year: $79 to maintain net-30 account credit terms, with an initial credit limit of $1,000 (there's also an option to pay $49 - $149 per month and get an initial credit limit of up to $12,000)

Credit bureaus where transactions are reported:

- Equifax Business
- Creditsafe

Beneficial for businesses in these industries:

- B2B companies
- Nonprofits

8. Office Garner

From office supplies and electronics to apparel and branded business cards and websites, Office Garner has everything small business owners need to get off the ground.

They have a simple one-time $69 fee to participate in their net-30 program (rather than a recurring annual fee).

And with reasonable eligibility requirements of operating in the US, being in business for just 30 days, and having a clean business history, Office Garner is a net-30 vendor many companies will be interested in.

Minimum orders needed to report to the credit bureau: $45

Membership fee per year: A one-time fee of $69 to maintain 30-day net terms

Credit bureaus where transactions are reported:

- Equifax Business
- Creditsafe

Beneficial for businesses in these industries:

- B2B
- Startups
- E-commerce businesses

9. Newegg Business

Some of Newegg Business's product categories include: computers, electronics, office supplies, networking solutions, and digital signage.

Therefore, there are several products you can conveniently purchase from Newegg Business to run your company while also building business credit and raising your credit score.

Applying for a net-30 account is straightforward. You simply need to have a registered business name and address, federal tax ID, DUNS number, and a Newegg Business account.

Minimum orders needed to report to the credit bureau: $0

Membership fee per year: $0 to maintain net-30 account credit terms

Credit bureaus where transactions are reported:

- Dun & Bradstreet
- Equifax Business

Beneficial for businesses in these industries:

- Startups
- Education
- Healthcare

10. Wayfair

With a staggering 40 million-plus products, including furniture, appliances, decor, lighting, and much more, Wayfair carries a massive catalog for businesses.

An added plus is that they offer frequent sales and discounts as well as fast and free shipping on orders over $35. They also have excellent customer service.

Note that, technically, Wayfair has a net-60 account, which gives you 60 days to pay an invoice. But it's included here because they offer at least 30-day payment terms.

Minimum orders needed to report to the credit bureau: $0

Membership fee per year: $0 to maintain net-30 account payment terms

Credit bureaus where transactions are reported:

- Dun & Bradstreet
- Experian Business

Beneficial for businesses in these industries:

- Startups
- B2B
- Anyone who needs office furniture or decor

11. HD Supply

If you're looking for a large variety of products, including office supplies, appliances, furniture, electronics, and more, you can have them all with HD Supply.

They have discounts on clearance items and discontinued items, as well as other promotions, which can be especially helpful for small businesses with tight budgets.

HD Supply has no membership fee or minimum order to be eligible for net-30 payment terms, making them stand out against many other vendors.

Minimum orders needed to report to the credit bureau: $0

Membership fee per year: $0 to maintain net-30 account payment terms

Credit bureau where transactions are reported:

- Dun & Bradstreet

Beneficial for businesses in these industries:

> ➤ Startups
> ➤ Hospitality
> ➤ Healthcare

12. Strategic Network Solutions

Strategic Network Solutions focuses on four main types of business services—business continuity, disaster recovery, endpoint security, and proactive support. Besides that, they carry computer accessories and office supplies, for well-rounded offerings.

To qualify, you must spend at least $90 on a downloadable product, and Strategic Network Solutions will give you a $2,000 credit limit on a net-30 account.

Minimum orders needed to report to the credit bureau: $90

Membership fee per year: $0 to maintain net-30 account payment terms

Credit bureaus where transactions are reported:

- Experian Business
- Creditsafe

Beneficial for businesses in these industries:

- E-commerce businesses
- B2B
- Startups

13. SupplyWorks

With SupplyWorks, you can find a nice selection of cleaning/ janitorial, paper, HVAC, and lighting products while also increasing cash flow and raising your business credit score. Therefore, this vendor can be a good option when it comes to the nuts and bolts of running a brick-and-mortar.

The only downside is their $150 minimum order is higher than many other net-30 vendors, and they don't disclose which business credit bureaus they report to.

Minimum orders needed to report to the credit bureau: $150

Membership fee per year: $0 to maintain net-30 account credit terms

Credit bureau where transactions are reported is not disclosed.

Beneficial for businesses in these industries:

- Any brick-and-mortar business
- Hospitality
- Healthcare
- Education

14. Staples

As one of the world's leading suppliers of office products, Staples needs no introduction, and they're a consistent favorite among many business owners.

Besides office supplies, they also carry computers, electronics, printers, cleaning supplies, and more, making Staples a true one-stop shop. An added plus is that Staples gives you 5% back on purchases, and they have great customer service.

Minimum orders needed to report to the credit bureau: $0

Membership fee per year: $79–$299 per year, depending on the membership tier to maintain net-30 account credit terms

Business credit bureau reporting to:

- Dun & Bradstreet

Beneficial for businesses in these industries:

- Ten or more employees
- Any brick-and-mortar business
- Retail
- Education

15. Laughlin and Associates

Finally, Laughlin and Associates provide several business services, including accounting, taxes, compliance assistance, name changes, and trademark acquisition.

This makes this net-30 vendor ideal for startups that want to build credit while getting professional assistance during the initial business formation stages.

As long as you have a business bank account, a DUNS number, and are in good standing with the Secretary of State, you should be eligible for a net-30 account with Laughlin and Associates.

Minimum orders needed to report to the credit bureau: $0

Membership fee per year: $99 to maintain net-30 account payment terms

Credit bureaus where transactions are reported:

- Equifax Business
- Experian Business

Beneficial for businesses in these industries:

- Startups
- E-commerce businesses
- Most companies in the business formation stage

SUMMARY

The perfect business structure

Different types of legal structures for your business

What EIN-only business credit really is

Building business credit (EIN only)

Purchase/lease a vehicle

How to start a gas card rental business

Dealership list

List of recommended no PG banks

Dealing with the dealership

The end/your new beginning

BUSINESS VEHICLE EIN ONLY

Business Development & No PG Business Credit
Patrice S. Jordan, No PG Business Credit Consultant
Address: 6543 S. Las Vegas Blvd., Las Vegas, NV 89119
Phone: 844-478-2858
www.bossesbuildbusinesscredit.com

To order additional copies of *Business Vehicle EIN Only*:
www.Patricebookoffer.com
Bulk orders are available!

Patrice is available for One-on-One Business Coaching and
Consultations as well as speaking engagements, seminars, and
workshops. **Book Patrice S. Jordan for a Speaking Event:**
Bookings@patricesjordan.com
www.patricesjordan.com

YOUTUBE

BOOKINGS

SCAN ME

www.ingramcontent.com/pod-product-compliance
Lightning Source LLC
Chambersburg PA
CBHW072209090426

42740CB00012B/2447